One Breath at a Time

Finding Solace in Faith

SALATU E. SULE

KUBE
PUBLISHING

One Breath at a Time: Finding Solace in Faith

First published in England by
Kube Publishing Ltd,
Markfield Conference Centre, Ratby Lane,
Markfield, Leicestershire, LE67 9SY, United Kingdom
Tel: +44 (0) 1530 249230
Website: www.kubepublishing.com
Email: info@kubepublishing.com

Cataloguing-in-Publication Data is available from the British Library

ISBN Paperback: 978-1-84774-167-7
ISBN Ebook: 978-1-84774-168-4

Cover Design and internal design concept: Jannah Haque
Typesetting: LiteBook Prepress Services
Printed by: Elma Basım

Dedication

For Nura Udu (1979 - 2011) and Dhakir Udu (2010)
May you be granted high stations in paradise;
For our families who grieved and still grieve;
For two women whose personal stories of grief gave me strength;
and everyone who has been touched by adversity.

Table of Contents

Acknowledgements

While writing this book, I stalled many times because it was too hard to go on. I am grateful that I finished and thankful for the support I received along the way.

I thank Allah whose words gave me solace when I reached low points. He gave me insights which helped me see the meaning in death and life.

"Whoever does not thank people has not thanked God" according to a well-known hadith in the collection of Ahmad.

Therefore, gratitude to Him is insufficient if I don't acknowledge those around me whose contributions led to the book being written.

So, I say, 'May Allah reward you abundantly' to the following:

Halima S. Abubakar, my sister-friend, who carefully read the drafts and gave me valuable feedback on how the words felt, hard as it was for her because she grieved too when Dhakir died and when Nura died.

Nuruddeen Lemu, my husband, who has always given me thoughtful counsel and unflinching support in every undertaking of mine, this book included.

Haleemah O. Ahmad who edited the final draft.

My gratitude goes to Allah for the strength He gave me, one breath at a time, during those difficult times; and for the insights He gave me so that I could make meaning of grief.

Simple Dreams

When I was a teenager, I had dreams of my future life. I would get a degree, get a nice job, marry a nice man and have children: two boys and two girls. Uncomplicated and neat, these dreams were as devoid of details as they were of trauma, upheavals or death.

Like many people, the life I imagined was clear, simple, and nice. Now I look back on my life and I see the many things, both pleasant and unpleasant, that I hadn't dreamt of—such as death. The only death I foresaw in my teenage imagination was my own death at a ripe old age.

Death was a distant thing that occasionally crossed the edges of my imagination. Acquaintances and relatives had died but I wasn't close to any of them. My parents are in their seventies, both are alive and quite healthy for their age. I am the fourth child of six—all my siblings are alive too; some of them have spouses and kids who are also all alive. So, when death did come out from the fringes of my existence to stand close to me, it was a strange feature on the canvas of my life.

We each have an inner world, a mental landscape which we subconsciously build from the experiences, people, and things that make up our lives. We include our plans, expectations and aspirations. In that inner world these are as real as the daily encounters we have. All the experiences, people, things, plans, and aspirations which mean the most to us stand in the foreground, like precious landmarks that give us a sense of stability, purpose, and direction. When we lose one of these major landmarks our world shifts massively.

Handling the effects of a loved one's death is one of the greatest battles our soul will ever face. Other losses which shake us deeply include divorce, loss of a limb or organ, debilitating illness, the crash of a business, miscarriage and a relationship which fails to lead to marriage.

In Surah *al-Baqarah*, Allah tells us:

> *And surely We will test you with something of fear and*
> *hunger and loss of wealth, lives and fruits (of your toil)*
> *(al-Baqarah 2: 155)*

Such tests naturally lead to grieving, which can be incredibly painful and lonely.

When I experienced grief, two women shared their experiences in dealing with loss. Their narratives made me feel less alone.

I hope that by writing about my journey through grief I might provide some company for anyone else in a similar situation. The lessons that came to me along the way might provide some insight into what to expect and how one might overcome the challenges inherent in living with adversity.

A major lesson I learnt is that the path is turbulent and sometimes desolate but it is not without hope, light or relief. One simply has to endeavour to keep moving towards relief, one breath at a time.

Verily, with hardship comes ease.
(*Al-Sharh* 94: 6)

Shaken Once—Now I See

DATE: *24th January 2008*

It is past noon. I hear the *adhan*, the call to prayer. I focus on it briefly. My main attention is on my unborn son. A short while later, I am anaesthetized, cut open and my first child is born.

It was evening when I came to. My son was healthy, strong, wide-eyed and feisty. I was in pain, feeling groggy and dissatisfied.

During the pregnancy, I had taken care of myself. I had eaten healthy meals and increased my daily intake of fruits and vegetables. I had avoided caffeine and rested a lot. I had also recited the Qur'an more, talked to my baby, prayed for him and, together with his father, named him Sabir which means 'one who perseveres'.

Labour had progressed smoothly until contractions stopped and a caesarean section had to be carried out.

I couldn't understand how it could have begun well then ended so poorly. How could I have missed his first cry? How could my first sight of him be through the cloud of anaesthetics that blurred my vision so much that all I could make out was a headful of hair and wide eyes? How could it be that I was unable to cuddle or rock him in my arms comfortably over the weeks that followed?

A lady whose sister was a patient in the hospital visited me; her sister had also undergone a caesarean section but had lost the baby. 'You are lucky,' her gaze seemed to say, as she looked at me and my healthy son.

Now, of course, I see that I should have been joyful at my son's alert eyes and full head of hair rather than be grumpy about my blurry vision. I should have been joyful that my mother, cousin, friends, and husband were available and willing to cuddle and rock my son instead of being unhappy about the operation itself getting in the way of my doing so. I should have simply been joyful that my son and I were both alive. Now, I see that. At the time I didn't see it, not straight away.

A little time passed before I began to feel that my faith was not as solid as I had previously thought. I had been shaken by a delivery gone awry. Then I had been startled and felt sad at seeing how easily I could be shaken.

I struggled to push away my dissatisfaction. I battled with thoughts such as: 'I prayed for safe delivery. Why didn't it go as I expected? Why do others have a better birthing experience? How can other women give birth naturally while I had to have my baby through artificial or assisted means? Am I a worse person than those fortunate women?'

I believe that when I asked those questions, I became like the person Allah describes in Surah *al-Fussilat*:

> Man does not get weary of asking for good but if ill touches him, he gives up all hope (and) is lost in despair.
> (al-Fussilat 41: 49)

Alhamdulillah, at one point I realized that I needed to get out of that zone of despair and comparison. I intensified my reading of books which targeted the soul, notably Ibn Taymiyyah's *The Purification of the Soul*. These helped me face my weaknesses and work on re-building myself.

Eventually I pulled myself together and began to be joyful again. I focused on my son's growth and health, my marriage, my home and my work. I was back living my uncomplicated, textbook life.

Shaken Twice—A Baby in the Picture

DATE: 23rd October 2010
PLACE: A labour room
TIME: Unknown

PAIN INTENSITY: On a scale of zero to ten, nine point five and climbing.
  I'm transferred to another hospital.

PAIN INTENSITY: Well above ten and still climbing.
  I grab the doctor's arm as she goes past the gurney I'm lying on
outside the operating theatre doors. I ask to be anaesthetised,
even though the theatre that awaits me is still being cleaned up
after an earlier operation.

PAIN INTENSITY: Well off the scale.
  I am laid on the operating table, beneath bright lights. I notice the
lights and the metal arms holding them as the doctor moves them
into position above me. I feel strangely reassured by those efficient-
looking lights. The anaesthetics get to work and I fall away into a
death-like sleep.

PAIN INTENSITY: *Unmeasureable.*
TIME: *Later that day*

I woke slowly and ran my hands over my stomach. Even though I was not fully awake my mind registered the bandages. I still felt some pain but it was overshadowed by the relief that the nightmarish labour was over, my baby boy was out and soon we would be able to go home. I asked for my baby and was told that he had been taken to another room. I couldn't stay awake for long periods of time.

Once when I woke up, I saw my friends and colleagues in the room. I couldn't make out their faces too well but they looked very sombre. I said something like 'Why are you so serious? I am still alive.'

Later that evening, lying in bed and still struggling to stay awake, I said to my husband that it would be nice to go home with our baby. My husband busied himself with something and gave a brief reply. Had I not been so befogged by the after-effects of the anaesthetics I would have sensed that something was wrong.

The following morning I was more alert and had stopped drifting in and out of sleep. My husband pulled a chair up to my bedside and broke the news to me that our baby had died during childbirth. He was dead by the time the doctors took him out of my womb.

While the pain of prolonged labour was tearing through me, I had concluded that there would be some physical damage to my body but the thought of the baby dying had never once crossed my mind.

I had simply been eager for him to be born so that we could welcome him into our family. In anticipation of his birth, we had named him Dhakir which means 'One who remembers God often'.

My husband had taken a picture of Dhakir when his body had been handed to him just after the birth. 'I knew you would want to see him,' he said to me. Dhakir looked asleep; he resembled his older brother a lot and had a birthmark on his cheek.

'He was well-formed, beautiful. He weighed three point five kilos,' my husband said. 'You did well, carrying him for nine months.'

During pregnancy, I'd done everything right—once again. I'd been more tired than in my previous pregnancy so I had rested a lot more. I had almost miscarried in the early months but Dhakir had survived up until just before the surgery. Labour had been allowed to go on for too long and he had given up before getting a chance to take his first breath.

So, after nine months of the stress of pregnancy and over twelve hours of painful labour, I lay on a hospital bed, a big scar on my belly and without a new born baby cradled in my arms.

Once again, my world shifted.

Anchors in the Storm

My husband helped me find an anchor by reminding me of something I had once said: that one of my favourite sections of the Qur'an is the narration of Prophet Musa's encounter with Khidr, where Musa saw how 'unfortunate events' cloaked beneficial things and that one needed to have patience in difficult situations.

Those verses became an anchor for me. I reminded myself not to fall into a state of dissatisfaction as I had done after the first caesarean section.

The hadith about the souls of those who die in infancy or childhood also served as anchors. One such hadith describes such children as being in a green garden with Prophet Ibrahim. (*Al-Bukhari 6640, 7047*)

> *It was narrated on the authority of Samurah ibn Jundub that the Messenger of Allah said: "Last night, two people came to me and made me get up, and they said to me: 'Let's go.' So I set off with them."* *He mentioned things that he had seen, then he said: "We set off and we came to a verdant garden in which there were all the colours*

of spring where there was a tall man who was so tall that I could hardly see the head in the sky. Around the man was the largest number of children I had ever seen..."

Then among things that the two angels explained to him was: "As for the tall man who was in the garden – that was Ibrahim. As for the children who were around him, these are all the children who died in a state of fitrah." ('Children who died in a state of fitrah' means children who died in a state of natural innocence or purity).

Another hadith states:

The children are the da'ammes (little fish) of Paradise. Each of them will meet his father or parents and take them by the cloth – or by the hand – and never stop until Allah permits both of them into paradise. (Narrated by Muslim, 2635)

When the child of a servant of Allah dies, Allah the Most High asks His angels, "Have you taken away the life of My servant's child?" They reply in the affirmative. He then asks, "Have you taken the fruit of his heart?" They reply in the affirmative. Thereupon He asks, "What has my servant said?" They say, "He has praised You and said: Inna lillahi wa inna ilaihi raji'un (We belong to Allah and to Him we shall be returned)." Allah says: "Build a house in Paradise for My servant and name it Bait-ul-Hamd (House of Praise)." (Al-Tirmidhi)

Fighting a Mutinous Soul

Knowing the promise in these sayings of the prophet Muhammad (peace and blessings be upon him) became my anchor but just knowing wasn't always sufficient. Sometimes I crashed. I would be filled with sadness about Dhakir—whose cry I never got the chance to hear. I would feel the massive gap in my heart that was never filled, that is, the space that I had made for him as he slept, ate and played in my womb.

I would imagine what it would have been like to cuddle him, bathe him, sing and talk to him; to watch him crawl and drool, babble his first words, play with his older brother, begin school. I was often filled with intense sadness at how close I came to actually holding him. He almost made it ... I almost got to hold my second son. That these things *almost* happened cut deeper into my pain.

Sometimes, I would wonder, 'How come I didn't have this chance to have my baby alive and with me?' This question twisted the unhappiness in my spirit.

When I felt this way, seeing a woman with a baby made me feel angry. I would look at the woman, who I had never met before, and resent her joy and her good fortune—by extension, I would resent her too.

It was a nasty feeling and I wished to be rid of it. I needed to act in accordance with my beliefs about the souls of babies who had died, to bring into my thoughts and actions the lessons from the story of Musa and Khidr.

I found that if I reached high when my emotions were that low, I started to feel better. I made it a point to say in my heart: 'Masha Allah. May Allah bless this baby and its parents, and all who know him/her.' Then I would smile and congratulate the mother of whom I was mutinously jealous. I held the baby and complimented the baby's plump cheeks, or cute nose, or bright eyes. I thought of Dhakir as a smiling baby in Jannah and this helped me produce a smile from the heart for the baby.

By doing the things that a jealous and fractious person would not do, the negative emotions withered away. By acting generously again and again I actually became much more kind-spirited towards women with little babies.

With time, I healed. The sight of happy babies and pleased mothers began to make me genuinely happy. I began to reason that if I had hoped to have at least four children but ended up with one, there was nothing stopping me from giving affection, love and attention to the other children I met.

This didn't mean that I forgot what I had been through. Indeed, I had dreams of the long labour but I couldn't recall the details of the dreams; the only indication that I had dreamt of it was that I would wake up suddenly during the night to find that I had tensed my muscles and held my breath—waiting for another wave of contractions to send pain tearing through me.

As for my husband, he had to endure the loss of a child and the trauma of thinking that I had died in childbirth. Some months after the incident, he told me that at one point while I was still in the operating theatre, he feared that I had died because of how long the operation was taking. That emotion stayed with him for a while afterwards. He would worry if he saw me over-exerting myself. Hitherto a sincere Muslim, he became even more spiritual. During *salah*, he'd often recite these verses of the Qur'an:

> *O you who believe! Seek help in patient-perseverance and prayer. Truly Allah is with those who patiently persevere.*

> *And say not of those who are killed in the way of God "They are dead". No, they are living but you do not perceive it.*

> *And certainly we shall test you with something of fear, hunger, loss of wealth, lives and (fruits of your work).*

*But give glad tidings to those who patiently persevere;
who, when calamity befalls them, say, 'Truly we belong
to Allah and truly, to Him we shall return.'*

*They are those on whom are blessings and mercy from
their Lord, and it is they who are rightly guided.*
(al-Baqarah 2: 153–157)

In order to focus on what was good about my life, I cultivated an attitude of thankfulness. Each time I said "*Alhamdulillah*" after *salah*, I would pause to reflect on what I was praising Allah for: my husband, our son, our home, our jobs which we loved, friends and family who had rallied round during that difficult time, my mom who had looked after me for almost a month after the surgery, and so on. Gradually, my world settled.

Shaken Thrice—A Stranger on the Line

It was July, a month famous for its frequent and heavy rains. On this particular day, it was cloudy and had rained almost non-stop since before dawn.

I can't say whether it got brighter later because by afternoon my inner world had shifted and I no longer noticed the weather.

On that rainy day, I was working in the office when my phone rang. I glanced at the screen. It was my husband's number. He had left town right after Friday congregational prayer to visit his parents, his sister and some old friends. I calculated quickly—he had been on the road for about an hour and a half.

The voice on the other end was a man's, but it belonged to a stranger. My mind quickly corrected the anomaly by concluding that my husband must have left his phone at the mosque where he undertook the Friday congregational prayer before setting off on his journey, maybe while performing ablution. But then I recalled that he had called me just as he was leaving the mosque, so he couldn't have forgotten it there. I thought maybe he left it at a filling station, but that would be odd because what reason would he have to take out his phone and put it down somewhere while at a filling station? My mind zipped from thought to thought within seconds, trying to tuck the picture of a stranger with my husband's phone neatly into the frame.

"Do you know the owner of this phone?" the stranger asked me.

I said, "Yes, he's my husband." Then the stranger asked, "Is there any other man there with you?"

In our culture, it is considered insensitive to give a woman or girl tragic news such as the death of a loved one directly, without a male relative of hers being present. This is an unspoken cultural rule which I had learnt by hearing and seeing things that I don't even recall, but that day, when the stranger calling with my husband's phone asked, "Is there a man there with you," I knew that my husband had died.

It was confirmed a few minutes later and my world shifted irrevocably.

Breathe

Grief is asphyxiating, literally. Shortly after that phone call, I started having trouble breathing. My mind kept spinning about wildly.

Several times, I thought, 'Call Nura and tell him something terrible has happened,' only to remember that the terrible thing to happen was Nura dying. Each time this happened, my mind went into a crazier spin. I felt like getting away but had no idea know where to go.

I began to wonder, 'What should I do? How am I supposed to handle this?'

'Should' and 'supposed to' don't help much because there is no procedure on how to respond to grief … there is no manual either.

Grief doesn't proceed in an orderly sequence, as we tend to think when we read about the oft-cited 'stages of grief'. It's a circuitous journey, repeatedly bringing us back to points where we have already been.

As I made my way through grief, I learnt that I needed to breathe, literally and figuratively. I often had to take deep breaths, hold for a few seconds then gently let the breath out. There were also many times when I had to stop trying to do anything, stop trying to feel a particular way. I needed to just pause and catch my breath so that I could carry on functioning. Hence the title of this book, *One Breath at a Time*. If I write nothing else in this book, I will most certainly write: 'Breathe'.

Don't Push Back

Within the first hour of receiving the news of Nura's death, I made a few calls: to my brother, Nura's older brother and a couple of other relatives. These were mechanical duties that needed doing. Once they were done I could feel my mind flailing, trying to grasp at understanding what had happened but not being able to. I felt very lost even though I was standing in familiar surroundings.

I really do believe that in those first hours, I glimpsed the edge of a mind that had broken from its moorings as a result of grief. I say this because after the first hour or so, I began to lose my ability to think coherently. My mind kept darting uncontrollably from one thing to another in quick succession. Words, emotions and pieces of thoughts clashed and collided within me like tree branches thrashing about in a strong wind. I became more and more desperate to get away from myself. I had a strong wish to run. Where to? I could not say.

I don't know how but it occurred to me that I should pray, that I might find peace there. I performed ablution: I washed my face, hands and feet, rubbed damp hands over my head. Then I stood in prayer; while in *sujud* with my forehead resting against the prayer rug, I said words of praise, before adding: 'My Lord, your servant has returned to you and you are the Most Merciful of all who are merciful.'

With these words came acceptance and submission ... and then I cried.

Calling out to Allah in your grief is helpful. It is leaning into your pain, accepting it, then laying it before your Creator. Even people who do not acknowledge the existence of God find solace in accepting the fact of their bereavement, which is unintentional submission to the will of God, for life and death are integral parts of the world which He has created. Indeed, to cope with bereavement, one needs to accept it.

This is what Prophet Ayyub *or Job* (may peace be upon him) did.

> And remember when Ayyub called on his Lord, 'Truly, adversity has touched me; and you are the Most Merciful of all those who are merciful.'
> (al-Anbiya 21: 83)

It is from his prayer that I took the words, 'You are the Most Merciful of those who are merciful.'

That afternoon, I took the first step on my journey to recovery by turning to prayer and supplication. This has become a habit. I pause to catch my breath in difficult times, I lean into the pain and call on God just as He tells us to do.

And seek help through patient-perseverance and prayer, and indeed, it is very difficult except for the humble ones.
(*al-Baqarah* 2: 45)

Call on Me; I will answer you.
(*al-Mu'min* 40: 60)

Losing someone we love is losing one of the landmarks in our mental landscape. We keep trying to put it back so that our inner world will again appear normal to us. Of course, this is futile because we are incapable of reversing time or reviving a soul that has left us. The dissonance so created intensifies the pain we feel.

Similar to this is the advice often given to someone grieving to 'carry on' as before, to 'move on' quickly, and to 'get on with life'. Well intentioned as such advice may be, simply 'getting on with life' is not always the best thing to do.

Trying to restore our life to what it was before, or to quickly move on, could eventually break us, like how a tree that fails to lean with strong winds will be broken or ripped up from the earth more quickly.

In order to move through grief, don't push back. Like every storm, it will eventually grow less turbulent and allow you to move with greater ease.

Day 1: The Next Few Hours— You are not Alone

People came to offer their condolences. They said words of prayer and comfort. Every now and then someone said something like 'You'll be okay,' or, 'It'll be fine.'

At first, I clung to these words, hungry for solace. Then someone sitting close to me asked, 'What is the time?' Another person said it was '... o'clock.' I realized that it had only been a few hours since I received the news of my husband's death, but it felt so much longer than that. I wondered desperately how long I would have to endure this deep sadness that sat upon me if I was already feeling crushed after only two hours.

When another well-meaning sympathizer said something like 'You'll be okay,' or, 'It'll be alright,' I wanted to snap at her. 'How do you know? Don't tell me that! You don't know. Has your husband died?' I wanted to ask her.

Alhamdulillah, the words didn't come out. I felt incredibly alone in that room full of people. I just wanted to stop feeling the pain of loss but no one could help me and I could not even articulate how I felt. (*Even trying to describe it in this book took me a long time and even then, I still feel I have not conveyed it adequately.*)

Then a woman whose husband had died a few years before sent a message of condolence. I asked her to come because I needed to speak to her. I needed to know how she coped, how she had survived the first day ... and the days that followed ... and the months and years after that.

Initially she balked, saying it would be too difficult for her. You see, to tell the personal story of grief requires you to revisit the emotional sites of grief, fetch painful moments and clothe them in words. You must push through the barbs of pain, sadness, helplessness and so on in order to show the person with whom you are sharing the story, 'Here it is. This is how it feels. This is what you might expect.' Though this may only take a short time, those are emotions you would not wish to relive unless it were absolutely necessary.

I asked her again and she agreed, even knowing how hard it would be for her. She told me that she had had a difficult time after her husband died. She said the sympathisers would leave soon and I would have to find ways of coping alone. The mornings had been the hardest for her; she had fallen ill a few times but no ailment was diagnosed. She had known that it was grief. It got easier with time, she said. 'You'll be okay,' she concluded. I believed her because she had already taken the journey through grief.

A few days later, when another woman who had lost a husband spoke of how long it had taken before she could speak of his passing away without crying, I started to acknowledge that, before me, many women had had to have grieved for their dead husbands, and many would have to after me—I wasn't alone, or different.

Yes, there was the added weight of having lost a child only a year ago, but I tried to remember that there were others who had lost spouses as well as children, just like me. Feeling this way began to strengthen me. Those women has survived. I resolved to survive too.

Day 1: The First Dusk

Night fell. Many sympathisers left while a few close friends stayed behind. I was given a sleeping pill but sadness neutralised it and I lay awake in the dark for hours. Time seemed suspended. At about four o'clock in the morning, I eventually fell into a brief and shallow sleep.

This was the onset of insomnia, the first of many bouts I would then go on to experience. Sleep was one of the things that gave way when my world was shaken.

When you walk through grief, something must give. In order to survive the journey, you expend a lot of willpower. Your willpower becomes so depleted that you have to let go of some things in order to be capable of holding on to other things.

It is important to identify what is given way and know whether it is something vital or not. If it is something you can do without for a while or a long time, then do give that up towards reserving your strength for more important things such as controlling what you say and focusing on staying sane.

I found ways of filling the hours of whenever insomnia hit. I would read, listen to talks or watch television. On nights when I did not have the strength of will to focus on any of these, I would cry, pray or meditate. For two or three nights in a row, sleep would evade me until the early hours of the morning. The backlog of sleep would be so heavy that by the third or fourth night so I'd fall into a deep sleep at around ten o'clock at night, long sleeps that would last until morning.

Insomnia was one thing I chose not to fight as I knew that after a few days nature would claim its due. I conserved my energy for managing my state of mind.

Just as physical exercise can cause muscles to tear and bones to dislocate or fracture, emotional trauma can cause emotional injury.

Insomnia was a symptom of emotional injury which I had to contend with. I accepted this fact and tried to breathe while I waited to heal.

This might be different for other people. The one who grieves will have to identify where his or her emotional wound lies and figure out what to do about it.

Day 2: Clinging to Hope

By the time Nura's body was identified, taken to Abuja and certain other formalities were concluded, it was too late for a burial. It was scheduled for the following morning. This made it possible for me to make it to Abuja in time.

I left after the dawn prayer, accompanied by some friends. About an hour later, I saw a car that looked exactly like Nura's car, it was the same model and colour. Hope surged within me. I craned my neck to see whether, by some miraculous chance, I'd see Nura sitting behind the wheel. Even though I knew that his body was in the morgue, I clung to hope.

Over the next year or so, I'd be filled with momentary hope whenever I caught a glimpse of someone who looked like him, or who was wearing clothes similar to his, or was driving a car like his.

Sometimes I was certain I heard his keys clink just outside the door as they used to do when he brought the bunch of keys out of his pocket in order to unlock the door when he got home. Whenever I thought I heard his keys jingle, I would be filled with a burst of joy and I'd think, 'He's back!' Then I'd remember where he had 'gone' and the fact that he couldn't, it was a place that he would not return from. The joy would disappear and I would feel a crushing sense of disappointment.

At first, I tried to suppress this false hope. I felt that since I knew he was dead, I ought not to have such moments of joy or hope. Soon, though, I decided to let the hope rise, I endeavoured to observe it, acknowledge its presence, before going about my daily business while it slid away on its own.

One evening as I washed dishes, a thought crossed my mind that perhaps I should prepare a dish of spicy fried meat because Nura would love that. Then I stopped short when I remembered that he was dead. I stood at the sink, staring out of the window, caught between the fantasy and reality. I dithered, like a balloon tied to a post, moving in the breeze but going nowhere. Should I halt my imagining or complete the thought? I decided on the latter. Rather than yank myself back, I imagined Nura's big smile when he saw the dish of spicy fried meat and his exclamation of surprise. Then I made myself finish washing the dishes, wiped my hands dry and got on to other tasks.

Just because a loved one has been buried or a trying event is past, that doesn't mean we will no longer hear echoes of the past. Our past is part of our being.

Some people feel that letting the past remain a part of you is futile; they think that is the wrong way to grieve. One thing I am very certain of is that grief is a highly subjective experience. As a result, it is deeply personal. Even when two people are grieving for the same reason, they may feel that grief and respond to it in very different ways. No one can tell you how to grieve. You need to figure what will break you and what you can handle.

Here is what I think: pushing back the reverberation of the past can put a huge emotional, mental and psychological strain on you.

When those flashes of hope and nostalgia come, breathe. Feel the emotion, acknowledge it for what it is, call it by its name—hope, yearning, holding on, whatever—then carry on breathing.

As long as you are not treating the flashes as lasting sunlight, I think it is okay.

Day 2: Saying Goodbye

Nura's body was ready for burial by the time we arrived at the morgue.

I held his hand. It was cold and damp, as though he had just washed them or had just come in from the cold rain. I acknowledged the fact that though the hand I held was his, his soul had left his body. I believed, based on the sayings of prophet Muhammad, that his soul lingered near and I hoped that he could hear us because I needed to say goodbye. I knew of no better way to do so than to share beautiful words from a book we both loved.

I recited al-Baqarah 2: 256.

> God—there is no god except He, the Eternal, the Self-Subsisting. Neither sleep nor slumber overtakes Him. To Him belong all that is in the heavens and all that is on earth.
>
> Who is there that can intercede with Him except by His permission? He knows what is in front of them and what is behind them; while they can grasp nothing of His knowledge except what He wills.

His throne extends over the heavens and the earth; and preserving them does not exhaust Him.

And He is the Most High, the Mighty.

I hadn't memorized *al-Baqarah* 2: 153–157, the verses which he had taken to reciting often during *salah* in the last few months leading up to his death so I asked a colleague to recite it.

It was reminiscent of those times in the shadow of dawn when we had said early morning prayers together, God's words filling the space around us.

Standing with others for the funeral prayer was also a time for saying goodbye.

We say goodbye to past lives, to failed marriages, crashed businesses, deceased loved ones.

Say goodbye bit by bit. Grieving is not a race or a timed task. One cannot side-step it or sprint through it. It is easier to take it in small doses.

You might be saying goodbye to a certain lifestyle as you struggle with the effects of ill health, or be saying goodbye to a life of financial ease. Whatever the form of adversity you may be dealing with, act is if you were a long-distance runner: breathe steadily ... and pace yourself.

Later that day, when an elderly lady said that it had taken her many years before she could speak of her husband without crying, I told myself, 'This takes time. Settle down for the long haul, don't rush.'

The Week After:
Communicating with the Dead

A few days after the burial, I returned to our home. I was glad for its familiarity yet I longed to escape the strangeness of Nura's absence which hung over everything like a mist. The entire house looked exactly the same yet it all felt so *different*.

His perfumes, clothes, shoes and books all remained as they had been when he left home just the Friday before, as though awaiting his return.

On many occasions it seemed to me that he had stepped out of the house for a moment, in the middle of a conversation, and would soon step right back in and say, 'As I was saying ...'

Was this really it? Not even a phone call or something? When people die, could they not be contacted, somehow? Could séances be real?

Death seemed like a solid door slammed shut in my face, keeping Nura from me. A blank door with no keyhole through which I could peer to catch sight of him, no handle to jiggle until the door opened, no way I could call out as one might to someone inside the house: 'I'm out here. Let me in.' The yearning to reach him plagued my mind for days.

Had someone come to me then and said, 'Here is how you can contact the dead,' I think that I might have jumped at the chance, or at least given it serious consideration.

Grief could breed desperation. Driven by the strong wish to escape the pain of loss by restoring that vital landmark, albeit briefly, in their emotional landscape, someone who loses their sight, mobility, health, wealth or a loved one, might be ready to do anything to bring back what is gone.

As my head filled with questions about how to reach Nura, I turned to an old habit—exploring the Qur'an and sayings of the Prophet (peace be upon him) for answers. My big question: how could I communicate with Nura? I found an answer in several sayings of the Prophet (peace be upon him).

> *The deeds of the people who are alive are reported to the dead. If they receive good news, they become happy and share the glad tidings; but if they receive bad news, they pray 'O, Allah keep him or her away from it.'*
> *[Imam Ahmad]*

Imam Suyuti (Allah have mercy on him) authored a book related to the states of the deceased and the grace. Therein is a chapter entitled, "Presentation of the deeds of the living to the deceased" [Suyuti, Sharh as-Sudur]. He relates:

> *Certainly, your actions are presented to your close relatives and kinsfolk from amongst the deceased. So, if your actions are good, they are delighted by it and if they are other than that—they say, 'Our Lord, do not cause them to die until You have guided them like You guided us."* [Imam Ahmad; Musnad from Anas with some weakness in the chain of narration]

> *He also relates: Abu Ayyub (Allah be pleased with him) said: "Your actions are presented to the deceased. If they see good they are happy and delighted and they say this is from Your immense favour upon your servant so complete it. If they see evil they say, "Our Lord, reject it!"* [Ibn Abi Dunya; al-Munamati]

> *He relates from Nu'man bin Bashir, who said: "I heard the messenger of Allah (peace and blessings*

---

* *The report was cited only by Imam Ahmad and declared weak by Al-Albaani's in his book Dha'eef Al-Jaami', and he later corrected his view and declared it saheeh (sound) in his book Al-Silsilah Al-Sahiha."* https://www.islamweb.net/en/fatwa/306412/

be upon him) say, "Fear Allah regarding your brothers from the inhabitants of the grave for certainly your actions are presented to them." [Al-Bayhaqi; Shuab al-Iman, Ibn Abi Dunya; al-Munamat]

I wondered what sort of news Nura would receive. That I'd fallen apart because he died? That I was unable to cope? What advice would he give, if he could speak to me? Once, when I faced a difficult situation, he had said, "Counsel yourself the way you counsel others." When we lost our child, he reminded me of my attachment to the lessons from the story of Musa and Khidr. Knowing these were the sort of things he would have told me have me the determination to follow his advice.

I am grateful for the saying of the Prophet that let me know that Nura was still 'reachable', though in an unfamiliar way.

I am grateful for the many verses of the Qur'an, especially the ones Nura chose to recite regularly in the months leading up to his death. They became his message after death for me.

You will be tested; call on Allah; those who die in the path of Allah are not really dead, they are alive, it's just that they are beyond your perception so stay strong.

---

https://www.seekersguidance.org/answers/islamic-belief/presentation-of-the-deeds-of-the-living-to-the-deceased-and-martyrs-and-their-ranks/

Their combined message about death and the dead helped me see Nura's death in a new light. I saw it as Nura travelling to a city somewhere far away where the dead live, conscious and capable of receiving news about what was going on in this life.

My Voice is the Loudest

The day Nura died, I was surrounded by people. The next few days were no different as his parents' home, where I was staying, was filled with relatives and close friends of mine and of his family.

When I returned home, one of my cousins spent a couple of days with me. My sister also came to stay for a few days. When I wasn't actively taking part in their conversations, I was listening and letting their words cloak me in warmth and familiarity. Friends and colleagues called on me. I received text messages and phone calls from people including some I hadn't spoken to in a long time.

After a while, these visits and calls dwindled. Life was going on. People went about their lives and I needed to get on with mine but, to me, it didn't look like mine anymore. I wished I could keep people around me a while longer but I also knew that I had to find ways to soothe myself. No one could sit beside me, comforting and encouraging me, all hours of every day.

I turned to prayer, meditating and self-counselling to support myself.

When faced with diversity, one hears many things from different people. Some of the things said by people are uplifting while some only accentuate one's sadness or make no impact one way or another. Whatever message people's voices might carry, none of their voices will be as loud or as constant as one's own voice.

The voice in my head became my tool, carrying on an internal dialogue and debating with the unhelpful things that I said to myself.

When I said, 'I don't feel strong sometimes,' I replied, 'You're still here, still moving, still waking to each day, still trying to understand, still coping with all of this … so don't ever believe that you aren't strong.'

I told myself, 'Stay steady. Stay strong. Have faith, wisdom and courage.'

Words and Labels

As the months went by, I tried to mind what was going on in my head. As I've mentioned above, some days were extremely tough. I had to constantly check my mind, gauge its state so that I could care for it.

I avoided taking on any labels that weighed me down. So, to me, I wasn't a 'widow', I was a woman whose husband had died. I hadn't 'lost' my husband—he had died. My son wasn't an 'orphan', he was a boy whose father had died. I wasn't a woman who 'lost her husband and son within a short space of time', I was simply me.

This might sound like so-called denial but it was really me choosing to describe my circumstances in plain language which didn't bear any connotations. 'Widow', 'orphan' and 'loss' were words which alluded to vulnerability and they made me feel sorry for myself. I was sad enough; I didn't want to focus on the sadness.

I believe that the narratives we choose and the words with which we construct the narratives are important when we are trying to breathe through pain.

What words do you use when describing or thinking of your situation or yourself? What labels do you bear? Many labels such as 'widow', 'orphan' and 'disabled' carry contextual or cultural meanings which could be limiting.

I preferred to describe the events rather than to wear long-lasting labels.

The Next Few Months: Breathe, Be

About a couple of months after Nura's death, I travelled to my parents' home with our son.

During my stay there, I didn't get involved in decisions about anything at all; my mom took care of my three-year old son—taking responsibility for his morning and evening baths, his meals, everything. I slept, I woke up, I prayed salah, I ate, I watched TV. I was under no pressure to 'keep my chin up' or 'get on with life'. I let life get on by itself. It was enough for me to 'just be'.

To 'just be' means to take every moment as it is, make no major decisions, even avoid making some minor ones too; don't make any effort to be happier or more buoyant or more anything. It means letting each day pass quietly with only as much activity or input from you as is necessary. Do the barest minimum which includes bathing, eating and the like.

Time to 'just be' is meant to give you the boost to move on as best as you can when the time comes. It's the stillness of a swimmer before he dives; it's the careful measuring of a tailor before he cuts; it's the silence as you gather your words before you speak.

You need this time and space to 'be'. It is not a luxury but a necessary part of healing.

If you are facing adversity or you are grieving the loss of a loved one, recovering from a grave illness, divorce or some other traumatic experience, you need to find a place and time to 'just be'; a place where there is no pressure on you to be or do anything.

I had my parents' home and a month or so to 'be'. Another person might have a sibling's home, or an aunt's, or even a hotel. Yes, a hotel room could be such a place because there you can afford to close your mind off to things which demand your attention and willpower and allow yourself to 'just be [quiet, sad, pensive, etcetera]' and take life 'one breath at a time'.

We sometimes rush towards emotional 'recovery', or are rushed towards it by well-meaning friends and relatives.

'Remarry', the divorcee or the widowed person is urged.

'Have another child' the couple who have lost a child is urged.

'Do this ... do that.' Advice is given aplenty, sometimes too much.

The need to get away from an adverse situation is sometimes so strong that you might fail to look carefully at what you are going towards, like someone so anxious to get away from someone or something that she misses her step and tumbles into a ditch.

Many people who have rushed into remarriage after divorce or after losing a spouse, have regretted their haste at some point later. When you are still feeling the strain of your situation, create space to think. Don't rush into anything.

Emotional Scars

The trip to my parents' home consisted of a two-hour road trip and an hour-long flight. As the date drew closer, I felt reluctant to plan properly, pack my luggage or make travel arrangements.

At first, I couldn't name the emotion that gave birth to my hesitation but I soon came to recognize it as fear. I was afraid that I would die in an accident or a road crash, that I would leave my three-year-old orphaned, or that he would die as well and that would be the end of Nura and me.

Human frailty, the speed and seeming finality with which a soul could leave this world made me lose the courage to get on that same road where Nura died.

I had always loved travelling. Being on the road felt liberating. A change of scenery always felt like an adventure. To be so afraid of death that I didn't want to travel was like another precious landmark being stripped away.

As I mentioned before, trauma and grave adversity leave us with physical and psychological scars. Fear and insomnia were mine.

A friend delayed her trip until I was ready to go so we could travel together. Even then she had to sit with me while I packed. We repeated this a few times over the years. She'd agree to leave on the same day as I did when traveling, even if our eventual destinations were different, then she would sit on a chair and chat while I packed. Just having her company in the car as we left town and for part of the trip took my mind off my fears

This fear also affected my driving. While sitting behind the wheel of my car, I'd have a flash of imagination of being hit by another vehicle as Nura's was. Or my imagination would replay its version of Nura's car being crashed into by the SUV, of his swerving away from the car. These imaginary scenarios hounded me, coming upon me while I was driving, robbing me of my equilibrium.

One day, after I had been out with my cousin, darkness fell as I was driving her home. Fear of driving at night flooded me so much that it was visible. My cousin offered to drive me home. I was greatly tempted to accept her offer, but I told her that if we got to her house and I still felt nervous, then I'd let her drive me home.

As I drove down the busy road close to her house, it struck me that though night had fallen and the street lights weren't working, I had driven a few meters with my headlights off, but no accident had occurred.

I told myself, 'You weren't conscious of your headlights being off so your fear of an accident didn't increase. Had you been aware, you'd have panicked more. If you can drive successfully on a busy dark road with your lights, you can drive successfully all the way home with the headlights on. If you drive with fear, you will hamper your judgment, you might have an accident, then die, literally, from fear.'

I dropped my cousin off and assured her that I'd be okay. 'I am just afraid, that's all,' I said to her.

With my words ringing in my ears, I drove home with no mishap along the way. My cousin called to make sure I was okay. Laughingly, I told her I was fine. I took a small step away from my fear that day. Over the years, I took many more steps away from insomnia and fear of death. Even as the bouts of insomnia and fear persisted, I acknowledged them and I acknowledged the source—grief and depression. I accepted quiet support from my friend and from my cousin, often spending some nights in the latter's home, surrounded by her children and her calming company.

I'd like to say that as I write this I am completely healed, but that would be a lie. I have come a long way from that day when I was ready to step away from the driver's seat, but healing happens in phases.

Redesigning my Mental Landscape

No matter what you are dealing with, life moves on. When it does, as it must, it will take you with it whether you are ready or not.

At some point you will need to move. You can't stand still forever. Your mental landscape has changed so you need to redesign it.

I knew that after I had taken time off, I needed to redesign the world within my head.

Pain and emotional stress come from feeling the emptiness of the spot where a precious landmark once stood. Find the strength to turn away from that spot and focus on creating other landmarks.

Do not attempt to replace the loved one that has gone by remarrying, having another child, pursuing the next available relationship or trying to resume life exactly as it was before the accident or illness.

If you were bedridden for months or years as a result of illness or an accident, life would go on without your usual input. Someone or something would fill the gap you have left, or the space might simply be ignored and a new way of doing things would evolve to replace you.

You therefore have to accept this and start thinking in terms of 'Now, let me …' rather than, 'But I used to …'

Before Nura's death, I used to go for walks after morning prayers. After his death, I resumed the walks but made them longer and more regular.

I wrote articles and sent them to *SISTERS* magazine, which published them.

I signed up for online courses. I was redesigning my life, aligning my focus with what was with me and ahead of me, so as to give me less time to dwell on what was past.

I knew that there was no going back to things as they were before. The landscape of my life had shifted, things had changed and I had changed. I knew that I could find goodness in the altered landscape— and now I *have* found goodness.

When your life changes in this way, you need to follow the new direction of your life's journey. To do this, you will have to give a lot of yourself and you will restrain and push yourself in turns.

Find new interests. Immerse yourself in something positive, especially if it involves doing something for someone else.

I found that when I focused on giving time, effort or attention to someone else, the sadness that I felt reduced. It is one of the best therapies for grief and depression, and science bears witness to this.

As I mentioned above in the 'Shaken Twice-A Baby in the Picture' chapter, seeing a woman with a baby made me envious, but then this then helped when I learned to make pleasant comments about the baby and prayed for the mother and child.

This experience showed me that nothing beats back envy, self-pity, and lamentation better than praying for others and to sincerely wish them well. Wishing people well can be done even when you don't really feel like it but the sincerity comes eventually when you keep your intention constant.

I think about the Prophet's teaching that when we pray for others, the angels pray for us. I feel as though angels prayed for me too when I prayed for those who had what I didn't. I feel that their prayers were answered; I know that I started to feel better with time.

Seeking Solace—Calling out to Allah

I talked to myself about overcoming fear. I recited verses of the Qur'an and reflected on the meaning of the words I was reciting and I reminded myself of the lessons taught in the Qur'an.

I'd say to myself. 'You are strong, Salatu, strong enough to handle this, because *la yukallifullahu nafsan illa wus aha*. (Allah does not place on any soul a burden greater than it can bear – *al-Baqarah* 2: 255). Allah has given you the strength for this otherwise He wouldn't have permitted it to happen; He is not unjust.'

I took the following verse to heart.

> *Seek help through patient-perseverance and prayer; and it is truly difficult except for those who are humbly submissive. (al-Baqarah 2: 45)*

To exercise *sabr* (patient perseverance) is to stay steady even though the journey through adversity and grief is difficult. It is refusing to seek shortcuts and to be ready for the long haul.

It helped me a lot when I performed *nafilah* prayers shortly after I learnt of Nura's death. I repeated such *nafilah* many times in the months that followed, especially when sleep eluded me and sadness was all I could feel. My crying was often done in *sujud*. I would repeat this dua in *sujud*.

I recall that in the story of Yusuf (may peace be upon him), after Yusuf's brothers lied to their father that Yusuf had been killed, he said to them:

> *'I complain of my grief and sorrow only to Allah'*
> *(Yusuf 12: 86)*

Also, the statement of Prophet Ayyub (may peace be upon him) to Allah when he was tested with material loss, disease and bereavement was:

> *My Lord, adversity has touched me. And you are the*
> *Most Merciful of all those who are merciful.*
> *(al-Anbiya 21: 83)*

I would repeat this dua in *sujud*.

Within the first hour of Nura's death, I had prayed: 'Allah, don't test me anymore. Our baby died, now Nura. Please, no more.' Even as I finished saying this, I realised that I was asking for the impossible because it's a given fact that life comes with trials.

Asking God to keep you away from trials is like saying, 'Allah, don't take my soul. Let me live forever,' when it is known that every living soul shall taste death. Or like saying, 'I don't want to ever be thirsty or hungry again.'

So, instead of praying for 'no more trials', I switched to praying for strength, courage, wisdom and faith to go through trials and to be protected from any evil that might come with them.

In my lowest moments, I would make dua for these four things; I would also make dua for Nura's soul to be granted light and mercy, reward for all his good deeds and forgiveness for his errors. I turned moments of deep grief and pain to moments of dua. Calling out to Allah was vital to my staying steady.

Seeking Solace—Listening to my Lord

In my early years of trying to understand Islam, I read the translated copy of the Qur'an. I wanted to understand what Islam was all about. There were verses I came across while reading the Qur'an, while listening to talks on Islam and when reading hadith and Islamic books, which gave me a sense of what Allah wanted for us, who He is, what attitudes we should adopt and so on.

When grief touched me and my world was shifted, I listened to God. I was strengthened by His words. Let me highlight some of them.

> *God does not place on anyone (any soul) a burden except what it can bear. (al-Baqarah 2: 286)*

I often said to myself 'If Allah only places on us what we can bear, and He has decreed this trial for me, then it means that I can bear it. I only have to trust Him, depend on Him and stay courageous and strong.'

> *Whoever is conscious of Allah, He will make a way out and He will provide for him from where he does not*

expect; and whoever relies on Allah, He will be enough
for him. Allah definitely brings about what He decrees.
Indeed Allah has set a measure for all things.
(*al-Talaq* 65: 2–3)

These verses had multi-layered meanings and messages for me:

Allah has set a measure for all things: The intensity of the pain has an expiry date; it has been set already and it will come whether you fret or not.

Whoever is conscious of Allah...He will provide for him from where he does not expect: Focus on Allah because the '*way out*' will be provided by Him for '*the one who is conscious of Him*'; the relief will come in ways one cannot predict. I needed to expend more energy on maintaining my connection with Him.

When I felt bewildered at the death of my husband, or felt disadvantaged by the bereavement I'd experienced, or started to feel sorry for myself or see myself as having 'lost' in some way, I remembered *al-Baqarah* 2: 155 where Allah said He would surely try us. So, I wasn't being punished; this is not a blight on my life. It was simply a part of life.

Whenever I envied anyone their having had children successfully or their having an enduring marriage, or felt pained that my second son had died at birth or that my husband died, I recalled *al-Imran* 3: 140

Such varying fortunes do we give people by turns.

Just as it had been my turn to rejoice at the birth of our first son, and to enjoy a happy marriage while others had none of that or indeed the opposite—bereavement, divorce or marital upheaval—it was my turn to see another side of life.

Whenever I wondered if Allah would answer my prayers, I remembered:

> *Call on Me and I will answer you*
> (*al-Mu'min* 40: 60)
>
> *Call on 'Allah' or call on 'The Most Merciful.' Whichever you*
> *call (it is well) for to Him belong the Most Beautiful Names.*
> (*Bani Isra'il* 17: 110)

When I felt alone, I remembered:

> *When My servant asks you about Me (say) I am close.*
> *I hear the supplicant when he calls upon Me. Then let*
> *them respond to Me and believe in Me so that they may*
> *be led aright.*
> (*al-Baqarah* 2: 186)

I 'responded' to Him by reading and reflecting on His words and I kept hope alive that He would guide me through my grieving.

Keeping my Lord in Mind

When I was about ten years old, two of my brothers and I got into trouble. The trouble involved my older brother, who was eleven at the time, attempting to drive our mum's Volkswagen. He succeeded in getting the car to move slowly.

My younger brother and I watched the tyres to confirm that the car was really moving. My younger brother placed both hands on the floor for better balance while he watched carefully. We were so engrossed in this that we didn't notice when one of the tyres rolled onto my younger brother's hand. He started screaming and I joined him too. Our shouts attracted a neighbour who called other neighbours to help lift the car off my brother's hand.

My parents came home shortly afterwards. They hurriedly took my brother to a clinic. I was terrified of what might happen when my parents came home. I went to lie down, believing that if I was asleep when they came home, they wouldn't scold or punish me. When I awoke, my brother was sleeping beside me with his hand bandaged. My parents never scolded us for the incident.

On another occasion, when I thought I might be in trouble, I went to sleep. Sleep was always a place of safety for me. As an adult, I still use sleep as a place to escape to—I would take an hour of restful sleep over any analgesic as a cure for headaches or stress. I treasured those initial seconds upon waking up when I would feel refreshed and feel that some distance had been put between me and whatever the problem was.

After Nura passed away, whenever sleep came, it brought peace with it but only for a few seconds. Upon waking up, the first few moments of consciousness were refreshing. I felt light hearted and I wanted to rise and start again. Then, as I became more alert, reality would settle on me like a cold hand resting on my bare neck—there were some things that were so heavy that sleep could not provide enough distance from. It was like driving past a huge rock or monument—even though your car is moving quickly and the road leads away from the monument, because of its size, the rock or monument appears right there behind every time you look round.

Waking moments became very unpleasant. I wanted to get away from the heaviness of such moments. I stopped having my habitual afternoon siesta and, as I mentioned already, some nights sleep simply wouldn't come. On those nights when I could sleep, my spirit would start to sink shortly after I woke up. I needed an antidote. So, after *salah* at dawn, I'd sit outside on the verandah and spend time praying and meditating, gradually easing my way into the traffic of the day.

My favourite words of reflection, taken from the Prophet's practice, were:

> Asbahna wa asbaha mulku lillah wal hamdulillah (Muslim)

> [We have come to the morning and at this time sovereignty belongs to Allah and all praise belongs to Allah]

This was uplifting for me because it symbolized my readiness to step forward into the new day, trusting in Allah to help me get through it.

> Allahumma ma asbaha bi min ni'matin aw bi ahadin min khalqika, fa minka wahdak, la sharikalak; fa lakalhamdu walakashukur [Abu Dawud, al-Nasa'i]

> O Allah, whichever of Your favours I wake up to meet, or any of Your creation (wakes up to meet, such favour) is from You alone, You have no partner: so to You belong all praise and to You belongs all thanks.

This dua turned my attention to the blessings that I did have. This was particularly helpful because for a while, I became hesitant about mentioning my blessings in prayer or meditation. I had developed the fear that if I focused on them, Allah would take them away to test me. I started feeling this way after Nura died.

Pausing to reflect on the bounties in my life got me back into a thankful frame of mind and gradually erased my apprehension of losing more of what I loved.

I also learnt over time to find the blessings in the moment, not just in the big and seemingly permanent things but even in those small and fleeting things such as the wind upon my face, a memory of a happy time, the strength I feel in my limbs as I take my morning walks, for example.

Even the happy laughter of some random stranger glimpsed as I drove past them became a blessing to me because the lightness of that laughter radiated to me and I would smile too. As my cache of noticeable blessings grew, my apprehension about losing them shrank because I realized that as long as I took notice, I would always find blessings in my life.

There were times when I felt helpless, like I was falling and couldn't hold myself up no matter what I did. For these times, I had my 'safety net' prayer:

> *Allahumma rahmatika arju. Fa laa takilnee ila nafsee tarfata 'ayn.*
>
> *Fa aslihlee sha'nu kullahu, laa ilaha illa anta.*

O Allah, I depend on Your mercy. So do not leave me to
myself even for the blink of an eye; and make right for
me all my affairs. There is no God except You.

This prayer gave me a sense that I could be sad, depressed and confused but still be safe because Allah would not leave me alone. I could take decisions and make resolutions knowing that if I took a wrong turn, Allah would straighten my way. When I said this prayer, it became easier to breathe.

Hasbunallah wa ni'mal wakeel; ni'mal mawla wa
ni'man-naseer

Allah is sufficient for me and He is the best to take care
of affairs, the best Protector and the best Helper

I repeated these and many other prayers and words of reflection at dusk, when I couldn't sleep at night and when my mood dropped really low. Keeping Allah in mind helped me stay steady. I no longer needed to depend on myself for strength. I could let go because I was reminded again and again where my strength came from.

These duas were declarations of trust and positive affirmations of hope. When saying them, I would visualize myself falling backwards then floating safely, or standing still in a field with hands clenched then loosening my fists and opening my hands, relaxing my shoulders.

Why does it Hurt so Much?

When grief overwhelms us we ask, 'Why does it hurt so much?'

If I didn't love Dhakir, I would take his passing as a good thing. I would heave a sigh of relief. I might even thank God for not making me endure having a child I did not want. If I didn't love Nura, I would feel sad for his other family members but get ready to carry on with my life.

Love for someone who passes on will produce pain. They cannot be disconnected. To refuse to love anyone is to live a barren life. It is the way we are built, to form connections with others and to grow to love them.

Accept that having that person in your life was a great thing. That the time they were with you was a good time. Their death is one of the things that happens in life and your pain is natural, therefore it is okay.

Find the space, if you can, to be thankful for the time that they were in your life. Celebrate the life that they lived.

Prophet Muhammad (peace be upon him), spoke of the beautiful qualities of his first wife, Khadija. Hearing her sister's voice even many years after Khadija had died (may God be pleased with her) brought tears to his eyes because they sounded so alike. He felt the pain of Khadija's absence; he kept alive the beautiful memory of her life.

Breathe.

Understanding the Pain

I recall witnessing a hawk snatch a chick. As the hawk swooped down, the hen squawked loudly and ran towards the hawk but the hawk was already rising rapidly into the air with the chick grasped in its talons—gone forever. The hen continued to cluck in alarm for perhaps a minute or even less, then it gathered its other chicks and started to peck the ground just as it had been doing before the hawk descended. It had forgotten its lost child and was engrossed in the business of feeding itself.

If we were like this hen, we wouldn't hurt so much when faced with a trying situation. We hurt because we have long memories and because we are keenly aware of our own mortality, of being born, of death and of the space we inhabit in between these two events .

Those who rush into something new, sometimes do so in an attempt to distract themselves from the pain of loss.

Distraction is good for a while, just as pain killers are good when you are suffering intense pain. However, pain killers are dangerous if the cause of the pain hasn't been diagnosed. In order for healing to take place, you must slow down at some point, and listen to what the pain is saying to you.

During and after doing some rigorous exercise, pain tells you which muscles you used and, by extension, whether you are exercising correctly or not.

If you twist your ankle when walking and you feel little or no pain, you'll rub the ankle and then keep walking. If you feel a sharp or intense pain, however, you will know that you need to attend to the ankle.

While recovering from surgery, pain told me when I was adopting a wrong posture that might interfere with my healing.

The pain of bereavement told me that I needed to slow down and breathe; it also became my reminder to make dua for Nura.

I think that if we didn't feel pain after bereavement, not only would we forget the loved one who is gone, we would also forget about mortality and life hereafter.

Death and loss sometimes make us focus our attention on things that really matter and adopt a balanced attitude towards life, they help us remember that nothing in this life is permanent and that we are really all just travellers.

Let the pain become the reminder, beeping from time to time. When handled right, it will eventually become less frequent and less intense. Then it will be time to redesign our mental landscape.

When will the Pain End?

On the day of Nura's death, I wondered how I was supposed to survive the heaviness of grief that had descended on me. I asked, 'When will this pain end?'

Often while grieving the loss of someone or something precious, we ask when the grief will end, we want to know when we will start to feel normal or whole again.

Think of a race car and the circuits it makes repeatedly until the race ends. Grief feels that way: you'll start feeling somewhat better, then a slight trigger will get you back to a point you believed you had passed. A word, a sound, a memory or nothing at all could trigger a wave of sadness, a flood of tears, a feeling of anxiety or a bout of heightened depression.

In the same way that old wounds sometimes flare up and scar tissue gets itchy, grief can reawaken. When this happens, slow down. Remind yourself that this is normal for anyone grieving. Try any of the coping mechanisms you have adopted to get this far. It will pass and such episodes will become less frequent over time.

The scars will fade but their effect may remain even after the real pain has abated. It took about eight years for my bouts of insomnia to stop and it took me about six years to get really comfortable behind the wheel of a car. My anxiety about travelling has reduced but even as I write this line, I am preparing for a trip which I'll undertake alone and I am very aware of a layer of disquiet. I know it is a wound that hasn't fully closed, so I am breathing through it.

One doesn't side-step grief or sprint through it. One must slow down, take stock and get one's bearings. Remember: the landscape has altered so you need to move slower than usual. This is necessary though it might be a lonely place to be as others carry on with their lives.

With the right mindset, the right kind of reminders and company, everyone who grieves will make it.

Just make your way along your path, breath by breath, one breath at a time.

Asking 'Why?'

Almost everyone who experiences adversity asks 'Why?' We ask 'Why me?', 'Why now?', 'Why this?'

We direct the question at God, 'fate', the 'universe', people around us or at no one in particular.

Like the character in the commonly told story who is told to pick one of several doors or boxes without knowing what lies behind each door or within each box, when we ask 'Why?' or any of the other variants of this question, we are not quite certain what opening the 'Why?' door or box could lead to.

It could just as easily lead to the search for meaning and understanding of one's experience and situation as it could open the way to rebelling against one's situation.

This is the reason why some people believe that rather than ask 'why' one should just accept the adverse event without questions. While I understand why people hold this opinion, I know that the question needs to be asked. The mind frame from which the question springs and the mind frame with which it is pursued is important.

The day Nura died, I asked 'Why?' I asked God why He let it happen, given that Nura and I had led a simple life, our income was modest but we were happy and didn't ask for much from Him; we had lost a child the year before and had done our best to make peace with that; why, then, would God permit this to happen? I told God, 'No more. You have tested me enough.'

At first, my questioning was from the stand point of resistance, pushing against the adversity.

Pushing against an event that has already happened is one of the most unsettling and exhausting endeavours because of its absolute futility.

Declaring that there should be no more tests gave me no peace because even as I thought, 'No more', I also knew that I was asking for a life which didn't exist because we are tested all the time.

I asked 'Why?' again but this time I added. 'I don't understand.' With the addition of 'I don't understand' my questioning became a search for meaning and understanding.

I think asking 'Why?' with the right mindset, which means seeking for understanding and meaning, actually helps to turn the adversity from merely a painful event to one which expands one's thinking. For me, it was like being forced to stop focusing narrowly on my misery but to look up and look around me—to reflect on my life before the adversity, my life during the adversity and on life in general.

To cope with adversity, to survive it and to thrive in spite of it, the mind needs to be open and flexible.

Asking 'Why?' out of a desire to understand and to make or find meaning of a rough situation, is to open one's mind. That very quality of openness to learning is the same quality which is necessary for dealing with loss. It is a form of submission, acceptance and leaning in because you are opening up your heart to the reality of your situation and you are ready to move forward through the situation.

It leads to richer and more meaningful questions. I began to ask in my prayers and in my meditations: 'How can I cope? How do I survive this?' These questions, coming from the right mindset soon morphed into prayers: 'Please help me understand,' and 'Help me cope.'

'Why?' on the other hand, causes you to take a backward step, to stand stiff and unyielding. This stance doesn't work when one is walking into a strong wind, or uphill. I have heard from those experienced in martial arts that when you're engaged with an adversary you must to be ready to be flexible.

The adversary in this case is not the adversity itself, God, destiny, fate or the universe. Rather, the adversary is the wild bucking that your soul will do when adversity sits upon it. Your soul must have its space to kick and buck but soon you will have to soothe it and this is done not with a tightly coiled mind but with an open one, not all at once but gradually.

If you open up your heart and move with the situation, you will find the load much lighter. Ask 'Why' with curiosity, humility and openness. Answers will come and if your mind is open, you will notice the answers when they come.

What answers did I get as I moved through grief? What meaning did I construct from my experiences? I came to understand that I wasn't the first person who would grieve but that adversity and its attendant struggle permeated life.

I learnt to understand that struggling made it easier for me to understand the struggle of others so if I did not give others support when they struggled or try to ease their struggle, then I was not giving meaning to my struggle.

I learnt that bereavement was neither punishment nor blessing— they were facts of life—and that if I doubted this for an instant all I had to do was walk into a hospital on any particular day and ask who had died.

I came to understand that I could find the good things in my life or I could dwell on what was no more—the choice was mine and even though I was hurting I still had the power to make that choice—pain had not robbed me of my free will. I needed time to come to terms with making this choice; if I kept my eyes fixed on what was in front of me, what had gone beyond me would not hurt so badly.

I came to understand that I could survive this because it wasn't the worst thing to happen to any human being; that even though my trial wasn't the worst kind, it still hurt badly and the pain was not to be dismissed; that the pain needed to be tended to; that I needed to care for myself and allow others to help me in whatever way they could; that I could find my laughter and feel joy springing within the sinews of my spirit again. I just needed to pause, stop pushing back, breathe and move forward.

The Gift of Hindsight

There was a time when I couldn't narrate any part of my story except in small bits, carefully disconnected from one another and from me, so that they would not come to life and catch hold of me.

I was like a person trying to explain, while her hand is caught in a door, what she is feeling. At such a time if words did come, they would be short and disjointed.

I am grateful that I have finally written this book, having started and stalled many times in the past few years. The passage of time has made this possible. It has also been helpful to remember those two women I spoke of in the introduction.

I have remarried. I have redesigned my inner landscape and I am still redesigning it. My past struggles and present challenges have their place in my landscape, as do my present triumphs and future aspirations.

Everything is part of me, nothing is useless.

Whenever I encounter a challenge today, I think back to previous challenges and remind myself that when tackling the toughest of those challenges, I was gifted by Allah with strength. This I know only from hindsight.

Most of what I have written in this book is from the insight of hindsight, gathered from looking back.

If anything I have written rings hollow or seems useless or is just plain confusing, it might be because you are yet to reach that place in your journey where this writing becomes relevant, or perhaps because it *is* hollow, useless or confusing (*I hope the latter is not the case*).

In any case, I pray and hope that you will find something useful here for yourself or for someone else and that you will have the wisdom to seek to understand and the patience to wait for the insight that only time gives. I hope that you will have the courage and strength to breathe, to be, to move forward and keep thriving one breath at a time.

Personal Reflections

Personal Reflections

Personal Reflections

Personal Reflections

Personal Reflections

Personal Reflections

Personal Reflections

Personal Reflections

Personal Reflections